The Inner Road To Healing
A-Z Book of Positive Quotes & Affirmations

Valencia Clay

The Inner Road To Healing
A-Z Book of Positive Quotes & Affirmations

Valencia Clay

The Inner Road To Healing
A-Z Book of Positive Quotes & Affirmations
Copyright © 2016 by Valencia Clay
Published by: V.L.C. House of Self-Help Publishing
All rights reserved. No copyrighted portions or aspects of this book may be reproduced or transmitted in any form or by any means, electronic or mechanical, including photocopying, recording, video or by any information and retrieval system, without prior written permission of the publisher.
Printed in the United States of America

The Inner Road To Healing
A-Z Book of Positive Quotes & Affirmations

V.L.C. House of Self-Help Publishing

Dedication

This book is dedicated to God for inspiring me to write a book of positive quotes. On this journey of healing, I thank God for providing the resources to help me get through the darkest places in my life. Without God, I wouldn't be where I am today. I am thankful to see the light at the end of the tunnel. Father God, you are my Rock and Protector. Everything I do, I do it for you. Promise to make you proud! Love you for eternity!!

"Our light only shines, when we're ready to shine bright and out of the darkness into the light, oh what a beautiful sight."
Valencia Clay

Introduction

This book of positive quotes and affirmations was written to help you overcome personal challenges and pursue your goals, dreams and aspirations. Positive daily quotes can empower, inspire and encourage you to make the positive changes needed to live a happy, healthy and productive life. I pray this collection of quotes will touch the lives of others to inspire, heal and uplift on a mental, emotional, physical and spiritual level.
God Bless!

Adversity

Positive Quote:
Sometimes we fall down when adversity hit but adversity should never make you want to give up and quit.

Spiritual Quote:
God will never leave you in the face of adversity but believe in God's promise, His promise of certainty.

Adversity Affirmation:

I will never let adversity defeat me. I am brave and strong enough to face my adversities. My faith is more powerful than any adversity. Adversity makes me stronger. Looking back on life, I have been able to overcome many setbacks. I turn my adversities into victories. This too shall pass…

Be Yourself

Positive Quote:
Be yourself and love who you are, you've worked too hard and you've come too far.

Spiritual Quote:
Love all of you, that's what makes life great, chin up, stand tall because God makes no mistakes.

Be Yourself Affirmation:

I can be myself because I love all of me. What people think or say about me is not important. As long as I love me, including my flaws is what really matters. I can be me and accept who I am. To be myself means, I don't need the approval of others. I can be myself and enjoy who I am. I love and appreciate me.

Compassion

Positive Quote:
Rise and shine, put your hearts into action, it takes kindness to be kind with some love and compassion.

Spiritual Quote:
To live a life of purpose, we live a life of passion, showing God's love on the surface, filling our hearts with love and compassion.

Compassion Affirmation:

I will show others love and compassion because that is who I am. Having a compassionate heart can touch the lives of others. God blessed me with compassion to share with out. Sharing compassion is a reflection of my own heart. When I have compassion towards others, my light shines brighter.

Do your Best

Positive Quote:
Go about your day, put your worries to rest, and give thanks when you pray for doing your very best.

Spiritual Quote:
We go through the trials, our faith is put to the test, but as a child of God, we put out trust in Him and nothing less.

Do Your Best Affirmation:

I will do my best in every situation and trust that all things will turn out for a greater good. I will put my best foot forward no matter what the circumstances are. Doing my best is all that I can do. As long as I do my best, I will accept the outcome.

Ego

Positive Quote:
When our pride is too big, it's the selfish we show but deep down if we dig; our pride is what feeds the ego.

Spiritual Quote:
The ego separates and causes selfish habits but God only creates love and without love we won't make it.

Ego Affirmation:

I will work on my Ego because too much ego ruins relationships and I'm not always right. Ego looks down on others and tries to be perfect. I am not perfect so I don't expect others to be perfect. I accept people for who they are without judging them. Ego will push others away. I will treat others with respect and compassion. I don't need to wear a mask to play a role. I rather live a life of peace, love and happiness than have an Ego that stems from negativity.

Fail

Positive Quote:
Survivors don't give up, a survivor prevails, a survivor will try and try again even if they fail.

Spiritual Quote:
Life is a journey, on a journey we trail and days can get stormy but God's love never fails.

Fail Affirmation:

I believe in myself, even when I fail. I understand that failing at something does not make me a failure. It teaches me that if one way don't work out to try another. First chances don't always work out as expected. I will try again and again and again and again. If there's a will, there's a way. I will pray about it. Most importantly, never give up.

Goals

Positive Quote:
Don't procrastinate when it comes to achieving your goals but self-motivate and never put your goals on hold.

Spiritual Quote:
Believe in yourself when you have a goal to achieve, God will always help and when we ask, shall be received.

Goals Affirmation:

I will achieve my goals and if I have to face challenges, I will be prepared to do so. Challenges and obstacles will not hold me back. Setting a goal gives me a reason to wake up and face another day. Challenges are just a reminder of what it takes to aim high and achieve the goals that I have set out to achieve. I am a goal achiever because I am a goal believer.

Happiness

Positive Quote:
Life is to enjoy, too wake up feeling blessed and your joy no one can destroy because they rather see you stressed.

Spiritual Quote:
If you're feeling alone with a sense of emptiness, don't deal on your own but pray to God for happiness.

Happiness Affirmation

Happiness is a choice. I will not let unfortunate circumstances dictate my happiness. I can be happy regardless of what's going on around me. I am a happy person because I choose to be happy. Happiness makes me feel good and I like the feeling of happiness. Happiness makes others around me happy.

Issues

Positive Quote:
We go through heartbreak and could use a box of tissues but through our heartache, we can rise above the issues.

Spiritual Quote:
Don't let personal issues break your self-esteem and whatever you go through, on God's shoulders you can lean.

Issues Affirmations:

My personal issues will not affect my ability to see the brighter side of things. Yes, times get rough. Yes, problems can weigh me down but if I stay down, it gets worse. My job is to face my issues without fear and find a solution to the problem. There is a solution to every issue. I will face my personal issues and do the best that I can in every situation.

Judge

Positive Quotes:
Don't live holding a grudge, it doesn't teach us how to grow but instead of being a judge, we need to forgive and let go.

Spiritual Quote:
If you were treated wrong in the past, try not to hold a grudge, just pass it along to God and let God be the judge.

Judge Affirmation

I will accept people for who they are without judgment. I understand, we're all a work in progress. We all have flaws and no one is perfect including me. If I judge others I will be judged by others as well. What I do to others will be done unto me. Judge no one and I will not be judged.

Kind

Positive Quote:
Compassion is love, compassion is kind, compassion we should have more of and keep that in mind.

Spiritual Quote:
God is love; God is kind, from the Heaven's above for all humankind.

Kindness Affirmation:

Kindness is something I should express every day. When I'm kind to others, people reflect kindness back to me. When I smile at others, they smile back at me. Kindness makes me feel good on the inside. An act of kindness makes God proud. You never know what kind of day that person might be having. Kindness can brighten someone's day. I will practice an act of kindness on a daily basis.

Love

Positive Quote:
When you love yourself first, from beginning to end, for better, for worst because love first starts within.

Spiritual Quote:
Love is who we are and it makes us feel good so shine your shining Star as God commands that we should.

Love Affirmation:

Love is who I am. Love lives within me. God created me out of love. I love myself, all of me. When I look in the mirror, all I see is love. Love. Love. Love. Love is caring. Love is sharing. Love makes me happy. I love others. Love is all around me. Love starts with me first then it shines on the outside. Love matters. Love is warm and beautiful. I'm in love because love is me.

Mistakes

Positive Quote:
Mistakes we make, mistakes we learn from, so give yourself a break because everyone has made some.

Spiritual Quote:
The mistakes we make are like a blessing in disguise but God never forsakes and neither is He ever surprised.

Mistakes Affirmation:

I learn from my mistakes because mistakes teach me lessons. If I don't learn from my mistakes, I will keep repeating them and that's not learning. Mistakes help me grow and evolve into a better person. If I don't learn the first time, I will try again until I get it. Mistakes are like a test. If I don't pass, I'll have to take the test again. Eventually, I'll get tired of taking the same test. I want to pass so that I can learn from my mistakes and move on to the next experience.

Negativity

Positive Quote:
A negative mind-set, causes worry and stress, better yet, we end up doing less and it makes us feel depressed.

Spiritual Quote:
Put your trust in God, the negativity you don't need and God is willing to do the job if you allow Him to take the lead.

Negativity Affirmation:

Negative thoughts steal my joy and create a sense of worry and doubt. When I'm faced with negativity, I change my attitude and think more positive. When I think positive it makes me feel better and I have a different perspective on life. Negativity causes illness. It depletes my energy and drains my spirit. Negativity destroys relationships and keeps others away. I refuse to have a negative attitude. I have to remind myself, life could be worse and should count my blessings instead.

Opportunity

Positive Quote:
When opportunity knocks, try opening the door and if the door unlocks, that's the opportunity you've been waiting for.

Spiritual Quote:
God gives me passion to go after opportunities but I must put my passion to action and believe in all possibilities.

Opportunity Affirmation:

I am not afraid to pursue opportunities. I know the only way to achieve anything in life; I must get out there and let the world know what I want. What I want is an opportunity to pursue my goals, dreams and aspirations. I will not miss out on opportunities. If I want something, I must work hard for it. Nothing will ever fall into my lap doing nothing. I must get up and get moving.

Positive

Positive Quote:
Think positive indeed so negativity won't intrude, positivity we do need to keep a positive attitude.

Spiritual Quote:
God gave us life and to the fullest we must live, no worries or strife but to live a life that's positive.

Positive Affirmation:

I am a positive person. I practice positive thinking every day. The more positive I think, the better I feel. Positive thoughts give me peace of mind and keep my attitude in check. Positivity helps me see the brighter side the things. Positive thoughts attract positive people and things. If my actions are positive, my world will reflect positivity. Every day, I will practice positive thinking, no matter how hard it might be. The more I practice positive thinking, the better my life will be.

Quit

Positive Quote:
When you believe in yourself, there's no such thing as quit, because quitting doesn't fit in your vocabulary one bit.

Spiritual Quote:
Giving up is not a word that describes you one bit but if God doesn't give up, neither should you nor quit.

Quit Affirmation:

I will never give up on myself. Quitting is not an option. If I give up on myself, then I give up on God. Obstacles will never defeat me. I am courageous and determined to do my best. I am a winner. If I fail, I will not give up and quit. I will work harder and train myself to keep moving. To quit means giving up on me. I love me too much to give up. I will try again before quitting. I am not a quitter. I am a winner and winners have failed but never walked away in defeat. Quitting is not a part of my vocabulary.

Rise

Positive Quote:
Never give up, no matter how many tries, believers don't give up, believers get up and rise.

Spiritual Quote:
Give thanks to God when you open your eyes, God is the reason we wake up, God is the reason we rise.

Rise Affirmation:

I Rise because I refuse to stay down. I get up because there's nothing at the bottom for me. When I Rise, I stand up with my head held high. I'm constantly reminding myself when obstacles knock me down, I pull it together and get back up, ready to take action. I Rise ready to take on the world. I Rise feeling blessed and thankful to see another day. I Rise because I have a roof over my head and food on the table. I Rise because God has a plan for my life. I Rise with nothing but love in my heart. I Rise with humility beaming from my eyes. I Rise knowing that everything happens for a greater good!

Strong

Positive Quote:
Be brave, be bold, be courageous and strong, a brave soul can handle any challenges that come along.

Spiritual Quote:
Nothing can go wrong when God has a plan just trust and be strong, we don't have to understand.

Strong Affirmation:

I am strong regardless of my circumstances. My circumstances don't change the courage that is within me. I see myself as a brave soul who can handle anything that comes my way. When I face my fears, it makes me stronger and stronger. There is nothing to be afraid of. Strength gives me the determination to overcome and never back down. I am a survivor and I can overcome anything.

Trust

Positive Quote:
Have faith in your days is an absolute must and when you walk in your faith, in your faith you must trust.

Spiritual Quote:
Life can be unfair, life can be unjust but its God who truly cares and would do anything for us.

Trust Affirmation:

I trust that life will always work out according to God's plan. I trust all things will work out for a greater good. I trust my life is in good hands. Trust is key! I shall go about my day trusting that all goes well without worry or stress. I put my trust in God. When I trust God, I can live life with a happy heart. Trust in God and keep it moving.

Unity

Positive Quote:
Help is always there for change in our community and for those who really care; our hands are joined in unity.

Spiritual Quote:
God loves us as a whole not to be separated or divided, from the youngest to the old, we stand together, and we stand united.

Unity Affirmation:

I live my life respecting others for who they are regardless of race, religion and ethnicity. I've learned to love all people because in God's eyes, we are one from One Source. One Universe. We're all connected. We might look different on the outside but we're all God's children on the inside. We don't need to judge, or look down on others. God lives in all of us. I only see love because God is love and He loves the world.

Victory

Positive Quote:
To overcome is a choice instead of living in misery, now we can rejoice and give thanks for our victories.

Spiritual Quote:
God will always win, His story makes history, from beginning to end, nothing but glory and victory.

Victory Affirmation:

I will never let my obstacles defeat me. I am victorious because victory is all I see. God fights my battles and I know He will defeat the enemy. Patience is key and I trust in the end victory will be mine. No matter what obstacles I face, the end result will be a victory. Victory belongs to me. Victory is mine.

Positive Quote:
You're a fighter and a survivor, your strength comes from within and you refuse to give up because a survivor chooses to win.

Spiritual Quote:
Cherish each day, every moment we spend, in God's name we pray and every battle we win.

Winner Affirmation:

I am a winner. I choose to play the game of life like a soldier. I am not a loser regardless of what other people think or say about me. What matters is that I believe in myself. When I look in the mirror, I see a winner. A winner is what I am, regardless of my circumstances. I am a winner because a winner is what I choose to be.

cellence

Positive Quote:
If you want to do better and if you want to xcel then put them together to overcome and prevail.

Spiritual Quote:
Be willing to xcel in everything that you do, sometimes you might fail but God will never see failure in you.

Xcellence Affirmation:

I challenge myself to xcel in life. The only way I can xcel is to get out there and try. Xcellence teaches me to aim high because I have a purpose in life. My purpose is to achieve greatness. Xcellence is about growing so I can express my truest potential and capabilities. I know xcellence lives within me. I want to be outstanding in my actions and show the world my best work. Xcellence is what I pursue.

Yes

Positive Quote:
Every morning you wake up, the goal is to do your best, no worry, no stress, believe and say yes.

Spiritual Quote:
When you think of God, think of the reasons you are blessed and even against the odds, God is the reason we say yes.

Yes Affirmation:

I say yes to I can. I say yes, God is great. I say yes, I'm a believer. I say yes to anything is possible. I say yes because I love myself. I say yes to, I will achieve my goals. I say yes to, I will live life to the fullest. I say yes to healthy relationships. I say yes to, I can say no. I say yes to, I will have more faith. I say yes to, I will pursue my purpose and passion. I say yes because I can. Yes!

Zone

Positive Quote:
Why do we fear? Is it because of the unknown, or is it the negative we hear, keeping us stuck in our comfort zone?

Spiritual Quote:
Focus on your goals, keep planting positive seeds and let God take control, providing you with everything that you need.

Zone Affirmation:

I am willing to step outside of my comfort zone even if it's uncomfortable. When I step out of my comfort zone, it reminds me that there is nothing to fear. Fear is an illusion. I will never let fear stop me from trying new things. There is no learning in comfortable. Growth is about learning new things. Learning new things helps me find my purpose in life. Learning new things opens up doors of opportunity. I'm always looking forward to stepping out of my comfort zone.

The Inner Road To Healing

"The Inner Road To Healing," is about healing the Inner You. It's about peeling away those layers of negativity and discover your true self. You are a God/Goddess with divine powers to create and manifest the life you choose to live. To live the life you choose, you must be willing to let go of what no longer serves your greater purpose. Many of us are still searching for who we are on the outside when everything we're looking for, lives within us.

As you travel down the road of searching for who you really are, look on the inside and focus on where healing needs to take place. If you have unhealed childhood wounds, more than likely, those wounds have been carried over into your adult life. Unhealed childhood wounds can have a negative effect on yourself and the relationships you have with others. Unhealed childhood wounds causes low self-esteem and unhealthy relationships. To create healthier relationships, we need to heal past hurts of resentment, rejection, shame, guilt, anger, blame and victim mentalities.

We will never heal by placing a band aid over our wounds. No! We must provide the necessary treatment by getting to the root, to the source of where healing needs to take place. Awareness is key. As a child, if you were abused, neglected, abandoned or mistreated poorly, it can dramatically have a negative impact in your adult life mentally, emotionally, physically and spiritually. We can't ignore pain that lives on the inside because it reflects on the outside. Counseling, therapy, reading self-help books, practicing positive thinking techniques, meditation, joining self-help groups are treatments to help heal past wounds. When we make the positive changes needed, we can heal broken spirits and create healthier relationships.

Healing starts from within. Love, compassion, harmony, peace, happiness starts with you. Healing is a process and when you're ready to heal, God will be there every step of the way. God will provide the knowledge, tool and resources needed but you must be willing to put in the work. No one said it was going to be easy but in the end you will feel happy, whole and free again to live without regrets. Are you ready to heal, face your fears and take your power back? If I can do it, so can you. Good luck on your journey! I know you will RISE and overcome because

God is able! Have faith and believe in you!

www.ingramcontent.com/pod-product-compliance
Lightning Source LLC
LaVergne TN
LVHW052256070426
835507LV00035B/3075